Thoughts and Feelings

Thoughts and Feelings

Sharing

Written by Susan Riley
Photos by David M. Budd

The Child's World®, Inc.

Published by The Child's World®, Inc.

Design and Production:
The Creative Spark, San Juan Capistrano, CA

Photos: © 1998 David M. Budd Photography

Library of Congress Cataloging-in-Publication Data

Riley, Susan, 1946–
    Sharing / by Susan Riley.
        p. cm. — (Thoughts and feelings)
        Summary: Delineates things one can share and the effects of sharing.
        ISBN 1-56766-674-4
        1. Sharing in children Juvenile literature. [1. Sharing. 2. Conduct of life.]
    I. Title. II. Series.
    BF575.S48R54   1999
    177'.7—dc21
                                                                    99-22908
                                                                        CIP

Hi, hello. Yes, it's me.

I'm here to share with you,
you'll see.
Sharing is something
all of us can do.

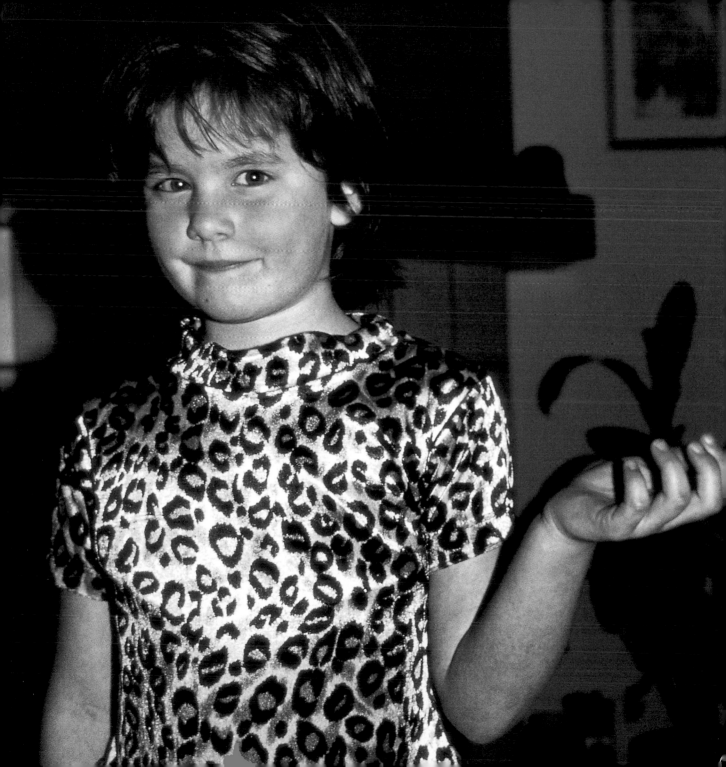

It means, "Some for me

and some for you."

You can share almost anything, anything at all.

You can share a book,

an apple, or a
bright pink ball.

Sharing your things
shows you are
kind. Sharing says,

"You can play, too.
I don't mind."

If you hear a joke or maybe a riddle,

share it with others and
make everyone giggle.

Some things
just have to be shared...

yes, they do,
such as hugs and kisses
and handshakes, too.

21

If you're feeling unhappy
or just feeling sad,

22

sharing your sadness

helps you feel glad.

I like to share.
I share quite a lot.
You can share, too.

You can share what you've got.

To show that you
love someone,
to show that you care,

just take
someone's hand
and say...

"Come on, let's

SHARE."

For Further Information and Reading

Books

Carlson, Nancy. *Harriet's Halloween Candy.* Minneapolis, MN: Carolrhoda Books, 1982.

Hutchins, Pat. *It's My Birthday.* New York: Greenwillow, 1999.

Lebrun, Claude. *Little Brown Bear Learns to Share.* Danbury, CT: Children's Press, 1997.

Web Sites

For more information about thoughts and feelings: http://www.kidshealth.org/kid/feeling/

Fairy tales and stories about thoughts and feelings from all over the world: http://www.familyinternet.com/StoryGrowby/